ELIZABETH
PEPPER
&
BARBARA
STACY

MAGICAL
CREATURES

The Witches' Almanac, Ltd.

Publishers   Newport

Address all inquiries and information to
THE WITCHES' ALMANAC, LTD.
P.O. Box 4067
Middletown, RI 02842

ISBN: 1-881098-14-1

First Printing September 2000

Printed in the United States of America

CONTENTS

Animal Kingdom   Tobias Stimmer, 1576

PREFACE

MYSTIC tradition grants pride of place to many members of the animal kingdom. Some share our life. Others live wild and free. Still others never lived at all, springing instead from the power of human imagination — many so vividly realized that we could easily identify them should we chance to meet.

Animals are magical beings, the subject of lore and legend from earliest time. Many achieved divinity and were worshipped as symbols of the highest virtues. Some were demonized by one culture and revered by another. Only certain animals qualified for otherworldly significance. Beauty, character, grace and symmetry were elements in the choice. And many possess a strange essence that clearly sets them apart from all the rest. We have collected their tales — our companions, the wild ones, and those wondrous fantasies that populate a world of delight and terror.

TAME CREATURES

If you really understand an animal so that he gets to trust you completely and, within his limits, understands you, there grows up between you affection of a purity and simplicity which seems to me peculiarly satisfactory. There is also a cosmic strangeness about animals which always fascinates me and gives to my affection for them a mysterious depth or background.

— LEONARD WOOLF

Cats

ANCIENT Egyptians were the first to domesticate the feral cat, doubtless breeding smaller ones to rid the granaries of rodents and venomous snakes. Innate dignity, independent manner, elegant appearance and affectionate nature soon elevated the cat from servant to beloved household companion. By the time the Greek historian Herodotus visited Egypt in 445 B.C., the cat was established as the primary symbol of Bast, goddess of pleasure and music, especially noted for her magical power.

The worship of Bast reached its height during the reign of Osorkon II (874-853 B.C.), when a magnificent temple to the cat goddess was built in the Nile Delta city of Bubastis, now in ruins and marked on contemporary maps as Tell Basta. Herodotus described the shrine and witnessed a festival honoring Bast attended by tens of thousands. He remarks on the "obvious antiquity" of the ceremony and equates Bast with the Greek goddess Artemis, for both were lunar deities and represented feminine self-possession. The Egyptian attitude toward animals particularly impressed Herodotus. Wild and tame creatures were all considered sacred, and cats were deeply revered. The spirit of Bast still appears alive in modern Cairo, where cats are ubiquitous. They roam the streets, hotel

lobbies, museums, mosques, shops and government buildings, everywhere treated with perfect kindness and infinite respect.

The ancient Egyptians so treasured their cats that exporting them was strictly forbidden under Pharaonic rule. Despite the ban, cats would eventually find their way throughout the Middle East and into Western Europe. Persians and Greeks also prized the cat as a protector of grain, and as such it accompanied Phoenicians on sea voyages and Roman legions on their conquests. Beyond its value as an enemy of rats is a certain mystical quality all cats possess. That essence is honored by some and feared by others. Time hasn't changed the cat or our attitude toward it. Someone once said that cats immediately recognize whether people like or dislike them, and never care enough to do anything about it. Perhaps the cat remembers its divine heritage.

Pagan associations would prove deadly to the cat as Christianity came to dominate the West. By medieval days felines were regarded more often than not as demonic, companions of witches and servants of the devil. Themes in Celtic, Teutonic, and Scandinavian lore further linked cats with esoteric secrets and occult power. The love goddess Freya's chariot was

drawn by two cats. Celts believed that a cat's eyes were windows through which an inner world could be explored. An 18th-century English witch described a ritual using a cat to cast a spell:

To be performed every evening, at the same place, at moonrise. Adapt your cat to sit close by you, facing the east. Stroke gently but firmly with love in your hands until its purrs and your breathing are heard as one sound. Now you and your cat possess the same will, your eyes will see alike, your thoughts will travel together. The time has come to work spells and cast enchantments, for power is doubled through the agency of your familiar creature.

Folklore abounds in cat tales with shape-shifting a typical motif. Themes from fantasy become frighteningly real when we read an excerpt from testimony taken at the 1692 trial of Susanna Martin for witchcraft in Salem, Massachusetts. Witness Robert Downer swore that the accused had threatened his life and "that night as I lay in my bed, there came in at the window the likeness of a cat, which flew upon me, took fast hold of my throat, lay on me a considerable while, and almost killed me."

A prevalent belief held that witches could assume other

forms. Reflecting it is a common tale with countless variations concerning a night-marauding cat discovered raiding a family larder and struck with a knife while escaping. The following day a highly regarded woman of the village is found to have a knife wound in her thigh. The stories of metamorphosis usually refer to women (cats and witches are most often perceived as female in folklore), yet one old tale told throughout Western Europe is about the King of the Cats:

A traveler passing the desolate ruins of an ancient church pauses to investigate an adjoining cemetery. As he crouches to study an old gravestone, his attention is caught by an odd sound — eerie yet somehow familiar. He peers around to see a curious procession of nine cats: one leads the way and the others, four on each side, carry a tiny black coffin. Resting on the coffin is an exquisite gold crown. The sound he hears is a kind of chant, for at every third step all the cats cry out together. The wayfarer hastens away to avoid being seen and reaches the home of an old friend at nightfall. In the cozy atmosphere of his friend's den, he relates the story of the strange sight he observed. As the visitor speaks, the cat curled up on the hearth becomes alert, stands up, stretches, and cries out: "Then I am King of the Cats!" and disappears up the chimney.

The true meaning of the cat's magical gifts may ever remain elusive. Despite thousands of years of close association, the cat is as mysterious to us today as it was when ancient Egyptians sensed its worth. A haunting feeling suggests that cats may know far more than they let on.

Cattle

CHARGING across cave walls and ceilings, deep in the heart of the earth, are paintings of great herds of cattle. The brilliantly conceived images are the works of artists in Western Europe during Paleolithic times, around 15,000 B. C. People of this era hunted the animals and presumably the cave sanctuaries were scenes of sympathetic magic to promote a successful hunt. Or perhaps the painters simply created memorials to impress future generations. The many bulls and cows depicted belong to an extinct species of wild oxen, remote ancestors of modern cattle breeds. Evidence of the earliest domestic herds, over eight thousand years old, has been found in northern Greece and Turkey. From that time sustenance no longer depended on hunting and gathering, for humans developed stable food sources by keeping livestock and growing grain. Beef, milk, hides, and the strength to pull heavy plows required to till uncultivated soil were bovine benefactions.

Ancient cultures honored the bull for his vigor, fighting spirit, and sexual energy. As symbolic of fertility, the bull became associated with storms of wind and rain that activated parched earth. Bull cults arose throughout the Middle East and India. As a female aspect, the cow represented the loving mother, provider of nourishment and protection. The sacred nature of cattle was firmly established. In India today cows in particular are venerated.

Apis, the bull god of procreativity, was worshipped in Memphis, Egypt's ancient capital city. Old myths declare the god was immaculately conceived by a ray of moonlight, his horns an emblem of the Moon. Other sources say a thunderbolt descended upon a heavenly cow and brought forth Apis, a calf of solar power. Hathor, goddess of love, happiness, dance and music, was personified as a cow. An archaic deity, Hathor presided over childbirth. Both Apis and Hathor were portrayed crowned with the solar disk between two lunar horns representing the waxing and waning moon. Over many centuries Apis became associated with Osiris to form a dual god figure called Serapis by the Greeks. The worship of Serapis flourished throughout the Roman Empire, reaching as far north as York in England. Isis, female counterpart of Osiris, took on aspects of the cow goddess, often depicted wearing the horned crown.

On the island of Crete the bull defined masculine virility. Bronze Age murals of a bull-leaping sport suggest a link to Spain's ritual of bullfighting. However, the restored frescos of Knossos have a playful air unrelated to the dark drama played out in the bullring. The bull often served as a sacrifice in early Mediterranean religious forms. Christianity's powerful rival Mithraism featured the solemn slaying of a bull in its mystic rites, and it seems more likely that bullfighting is rooted in that tradition. Crete was the home of the mythic Minotaur (half man and half bull), guardian of an underground labyrinth, his roar responsible for earthquakes.

Greek myths record that the great god Zeus disguised himself as a white bull to charm the maiden Europa. A romantic tale with a happy ending, for Zeus carried Europa over the sea to Crete, resumed his godlike form, and they found contentment together. His vengeful wife, the goddess Hera, apparently never got wind of the affair. Hera herself had bovine characteristics, for Homer often describes her as "cow-faced" and "cow-eyed." Another Greek tale has the beautiful Io, a maiden who caught the roving eye of Zeus, transformed into a white cow. Both myths are credited with naming the constellation of Taurus, a zodiac sign ruled by Venus and especially concerned with love and its many aspects.

Nordic cattle-rearing cultures found inspiration for their warriors in the bull's fierce nature. Horned helmets of the

Europa and the Bull   Saragossa, 1488

Vikings survive as proof of the affiliation. Celtic tribes in Ireland chose their king in an elaborate ceremony called the *tarbfeis*. A bull was slain, roasted and its meat and broth consumed as musicians played and priests chanted incantations. In the sleep following the feast, a dream would reveal the name of the future king to the presiding druid. Ancient Irish literature recounts the tale of an immense supernatural bull, the Donn of Cuailgne. Magic cows often appear in Celtic myths, most frequently white with red ears. Herds of cattle belonged to several deities, notably Flidais, the Celtic equivalent of the Greek goddess of the hunt, Artemis.

The horned beasts captured the imagination of people from the beginning of time. The raging bull in contrast to the docile cow, the destroyer and the nurturing protector became themes for art, drama, and poetry ranging from tragic expressions to the gentle musing of Robert Louis Stevenson in *A Child's Garden of Verses*:

> *The friendly cow all red and white,*
> *I love with all my heart:*
> *She gives me cream with all her might,*
> *To eat with apple tart.*

Dogs

A LINK is forged almost before conscious memory, born with the comforting nudge of a cold nose or recognition of sympathy in a pair of nonhuman eyes. And so begins a friendship that will never be forgotten. To experience the pleasure of a dog's company is one of childhood's finest gifts, for we learn to appreciate qualities rarely found elsewhere. Total acceptance, steadfast loyalty, joyful spirit, and unspoken understanding are canine characteristics.

Controversy exists over whether the wolf or the jackal or both are progenitors of the dog, but all agree that the dog is the earliest domesticated creature. Dog and human bonded during Neolithic times. The dog's primary function in prehistoric tribes was to protect the campsite, home and fields from intruders. Skills in hunting, retrieving, and herding developed until the animal became an indispensable partner in survival and later in sport, especially in royal sport. Paintings in Egyptian tombs depict elegant dogs — slender, sleek, swift — accompanying nobles in the hunt. The seventh-century B. C. palace of the Assyrian warrior king Ashurbanipal at Nineveh displayed a splendid bas-relief of a great mastiff straining at his leash, eager for the chase.

Beloved and admired, the dog acquired magical associations throughout the ages and in an odd variety of cultures. In tribute, the ancients called the brightest star in the sky the Dog Star. Its other names, Sirius or Sothis, later would be identified with the goddess Isis. Hecate, Greek goddess of sorcery and Dark of the Moon, was said to travel with a retinue of black hounds. "Hark! her hounds are baying through the town," hailed Theocritus. Greek myths place Cerberus, the three-headed dog, on guard before the gate of the lower world. Roman household spirits, the Lares, were often joined by dogs. And with her loyal dog Garmr by her side, the Norse goddess Hel ruled the icy underworld of Nifelheim.

Teutonic legends tell of the Wild Hunt. On stormy nights the restless dead mount black steeds and with a pack of black hounds stream across the sky hunting human souls. Their leader is Woden or the Germanic sky goddess Holda. The lore would surface centuries later on Cornish moors, when high winds and rainy nights invoked the spectral Wisht hounds and their ghostly master. In full cry, the jet-black dogs sweep across Dartmoor and reputedly bring death to anyone unfortunate enough to meet them. The tale inspired Sir Arthur Conan Doyle's *The Hound of the Baskervilles*.

The dog's magical image increased when Agrippa, the great Renaissance occultist, traveled all over Europe with an enormous black mastiff as his constant companion. English court indictments recorded during the reigns of Elizabeth I and James I prove that "feeding and employing an evil spirit in the likeness of a dog" was a common basis for the charge of witchcraft. The dogs described were often black, but included a variety of sizes and colors — large or small, smooth or shaggy, spotted, white, yellow, gray or dun-colored. Anyone who shared hearth and home with a dog seems to have been fair game for the witch hunter. Fortunately, the terror of witch mania failed to diminish English devotion to canines.

The dog's role in folklore and literary fable continually shifts from dangerous to benevolent. There's a ghostly dog that appears out of nowhere to guide and protect a traveler passing through a dark wood or other treacherous terrain. When the journey ends and safety is assured, the dog vanishes into thin air. Another motif listed by scholarly index-makers is "Lean Dog Prefers Liberty to Abundant Food and Chain." A 20th-century example is English poet Irene Rutherford McLeod's virtual anthem of the "happy outsider."

LONE DOG

I'm a lean dog, a keen dog, a wild dog, and lone;
I'm a rough dog, a tough dog, hunting on my own;
I'm a bad dog, a mad dog, teasing silly sheep;
I love to sit and bay the moon, to keep fat souls from sleep.

I'll never be a lap dog, licking dirty feet,
A sleek dog, a meek dog, cringing for my meat,
Not for me the fireside, the well-filled plate,
But shut door, and sharp stone, and cuff and kick and hate.

Not for me the other dogs, running by my side.
Some have run a short while, but none of them would bide.
O mine is still the lone trail, the hard trail, the best,
Wide wind, and wild stars, and hunger of the quest!

Geese

LARGE flocks of wild geese flying in V-shaped formation caught the attention of our ancients as the birds migrated south in the autumn only to return in springtime. Raucous cries from the geese announced their passage, true harbingers of the changing seasons. The Bronze Age drawing above is incised on a rock slab in a remote region of the Scottish Highlands and suggests spiritual significance. Norse folklore echoes the theme, for geese were traditionally sacrificed to the great god Odin at autumnal equinox.

A creation myth cherished by ancient Egyptians relates how Geb, the male earth deity, held the sky goddess Nut in loving embrace until rudely separated by a strong blast from Shu, god of winds. The concept of a masculine form for earth is unusual, as is the choice of a goose to symbolically represent Geb, one of Egypt's earliest gods. Egyptians were close observers of nature. Did they note the process of imprinting, especially apparent in geese? Newly hatched goslings identify as nurturer the first moving object they see. The response to movement as the source of nourishment and protection reveals a profound truth about life on earth. Far away in time and place, Native Americans associated geese with the earth.

Classical myths honored the goose as sacred to Zeus/Jupiter and Aphrodite/Venus. And there's a famous tale about the geese that saved the garrison atop Capitoline Hill during Gaul's attack on Rome in 390 B.C. Around the precincts of the Temple of Jupiter, close to the crown of the hill, sacred geese stood guard. Fierce caretakers, geese are attentive to the slightest change in their environment. Scarcely had the Gallic warriors assembled for their assault before the geese trumpeted alarm, rising up and wildly flapping their wings to ward off the intruders. Aroused in time, the defenders won that battle. Geese still stand guard in some locales, sometimes more effectively than dogs or electronic warning systems.

Divinities are often depicted riding geese in many diverse cultures. Brahma rides the cosmic gander in the art of southern India. Aphrodite, Greek goddess of love, is shown riding a goose on a fifth-century B.C. plate. The goddess Kosenko, borne by a goose in flight, is the subject of a lovely 18th-century Japanese print.

The favorite nursery character of Mother Goose has been linked to ancient goddess worship. Yet a bit of French royal gossip may be the true answer to her origin. Whispers had long flown around the court of Louis XIV that his queen, the naive Marie Theresa, had webbed feet. The rumor gave rise to an affectionate if patronizing nickname, Mother Goose. The first published collection of fairy tales, the 17th-century classic by Charles Perrault, carried frontispiece art captioned *Contes de ma mère l'oie*, tales of Mother Goose. How the nobles must have smiled behind their fans at the effrontery.

Mother Goose   Arthur Rackham, 1913

Goats

WE HAVE these antic animals to thank for their nutritious milk, tangy cheese, and fine wools, including cashmere. Beyond these prosaic boons, goats can lay claim to rituals of the highest order. Among the ancients goats were revered sacrificial animals, chosen for rites that invoked magic to gain the attention of a god. The ceremonial varied from culture to culture, but always there was the litany, always the knife, always the blood-spattered altar. Often the consecrated animal was roasted and consumed by the celebrants — death succeeded by life-affirming enjoyment. In Babylonia the priests wore sacred robes made from the skins of the sacrificial goats. As early as 1500 B.C. the zodiacal image of Capricorn was established, with its head and body of a goat and a fish's tail. The Sea Goat appears engraved on Chaldean gems, and a cuneiform inscription calls the goat "sacred and exalted."

For early Hebrews, the animal served in hallowed ritual at the Day of Atonement. Deemed Azazel, a wilderness demon, a female goat was chosen by lot and symbolically burdened with the sins of the people. Now ceremonially unclean, the hapless animal was driven into the wilderness to perish, the rite a yearly transfer of pollution to purify the community. Perhaps from this scapegoat practice arose a later tradition of the goat as a symbol of lust and evil.

In sharp contrast, northern Europeans revered the nimble

goat for its playful nature. The love goddess of Germanic tribes rode a goat to May Eve revels. She held an apple to her lips, a hound and a hare ran beside her and a raven flew overhead. Thor, the red-headed Norse god of thunder, drove a chariot drawn by two fierce, unruly goats.

But the Greeks, the most wildly imaginative of storytellers, had their own notions about goats. Zeus, "most glorious, most great," owes his survival to Amalthea, a goat. Zeus was the son of the Titan Cronos, gigantic father of the gods, who feared the prophecy that one of his sons would dethrone him. To avert the calamity Cronos simply swallowed his progeny: Hestia, Demeter, Hera, Hades and Poseidon. When Rhea bore another son, she determined that he would escape the same fate. She held a rock in swaddling clothes to her breast, crooning a lullaby. Cronos bellowed at the sight, snatched the bundle and swallowed it, clothes and all. Rhea then sent the baby off to Crete in the care of Amalthea, who suckled Zeus and nourished him to glorious manhood. Her name was given to the legendary Horn of Plenty, the cornucopia from which flowed all desirable things.

As prophesied, the army of Zeus did mighty battle with the forces of Cronos as the skies thundered, the earth trembled, and tidal waves plunged. The young god Pan hailed the combat from the sidelines, shrieking with excitement. His shrill cries instilled such dread that they finally helped to rout the besieged Titans — the earliest case of inspiring "panic." Zeus prevailed and his siblings, freed from their peculiar prison, adjourned to Mount Olympus and chose him as their supreme ruler.

Pan also attended Dionysus/Bacchus, god of vegetation

Aphrodite gambles with Pan   Greek, 4th century B.C.

and of wine, in ecstatic revels celebrating the pure joy of being alive. The fertility deity Pan is depicted as a rough, lustful figure with the horns, legs and ears of a goat, and he often turns up with satyrs, also goat-men. Pan haunted pastures and enjoyed making people as well as cattle stampede in "panic." Twice yearly devotees of the nature cult whipped themselves into orgiastic frenzies of inspiration and of mystical ecstasy. The *orgia* invoked the cultists' unbridled animal nature and freedom from man-made restraints.

The revels reflected the dual nature of the god of wine, sometimes inspiring, sometimes unleashing dark forces. Beyond the wildness the woodland worship was simpler, providing adherents with relief from dusty city streets and hard labor. Living on herbs and berries, drinking from clear pools and sleeping on soft grass, the celebrants were renewed by the purity and beauty of the natural world. Four days later they would return refreshed to their families.

Oddly enough, we owe the art of drama to the Athenian music and dance festivals honoring Dionysus, whose symbol was the goat. The chorus and dancers wore goatskins and rites were traditionally orderly until a singer named Thespis entered into a dispute with the choral leader. The audience relished the lively verbal exchange. Thereafter a priest served as a speaker and entered into dialogue with the dancers, who evolved into the chorus in Athenian drama. Aeschylus had the brilliant idea to add a second speaker, and true theater was born. "Thespian" entered language as a term for actors; tragedy, the highest form of drama, means "goat song" in Greek.

But high comedy by way of goats prevailed during the Floralia, celebrated on April 28th in ancient Rome. The holiday was an erotic spring bash marked by lascivious performances in the Circus Maximus. To add to the festivity, goats as well as hares, both fertility symbols, were released amid the legs of the crowd, their frantic chase inspiring hysterical laughter. Spring fever is an old, old story.

Hawks and Falcons

THE SOARING flight of a hawk is one of nature's most thrilling sights. Early Egyptians, observing the bird's dominion of the airy realm, referred to it as "God of the Sky." They named the hawk Horus and worshipped him before the dynasties began, believing that this bird's quality defined a vision of all that was worthy of respect and devotion. His right eye represented the Sun; his left, the Moon; the stars shone in his speckled plumage. Temple priests must have tamed and tended the wild birds, for they were depicted in ancient art perched on a block without tether, free to fly as they chose.

As the culture progressed, the sun god Ra evolved into the supreme deity. But the image of the hawk persisted in Ra's symbolic figure as a hawk-headed human wearing a sun disk on his head. The sky god Horus retained prestige by a mystical identification with royal power, and later artists added a pharaoh's crown to the hawk image.

Centuries passed and new legends bequeathed Horus to Isis and Osiris as their son, and over time the myth extended to portray the hawk god as the heroic avenger of his father. In Egypt, the hawk remained a spiritual presence in the sacred precincts of the temple, too revered a creature to be used for sport. The fifth-century B.C. Greek historian Herodotus visited Egypt and noted: "For killing a hawk, whether deliberately or not, the punishment is inevitably death." The hawk was the primary symbol of honor, dignity, and supremacy for over the three thousand years of ancient Egyptian culture.

Other cultures revered the birds as superb hunting companions. Hunting with birds of prey originated in China around 2000 B.C., spreading westward to India, Arabia, and Persia over a long passage of time. The returning Crusaders introduced the hunting tradition to Europe and the British Isles, where it found great favor within the royal courts.

Royal Hawking Party   Paris, 1493

The words "falcon" and "hawk" are used interchangeably, but in the sport of falconry sharper distinction is drawn. The hawk is short winged with bright yellow eyes; the falcon long winged with dark eyes. The bird favored by hunters is the female peregrine falcon. She is larger and more powerful than the male, as is the case with all the birds of this particular species.

But it isn't necessarily the hunter going forth with a hooded bird on his gauntleted wrist who experiences the richest pleasure of falconry. That must belong to those who tame and train the noble birds. One can imagine a spiritual kinship existing between the temple priests of ancient Egypt and their medieval counterparts preparing the birds for the field. Even today, the art is practiced in isolated regions where vast open countryside exists. Great patience, determination, and an intuitive gift are required to gain the trust and affection of wild creatures. This especially applies to hawks and falcons, by nature restless, moody birds. Long hours in darkened rooms, often late into the night, feeding and stroking the bird with a feather is the centuries-old method of taming. Feather-stroking is essential; oil from human skin can disturb the bird's plumage by removing a natural protective coating. A quiet meditative state, slow movement and soft words calm the bird during the process. And the reward far outweighs the effort, for the quality of an established rapport between human and bird is intensely satisfying — more than that, inspiring. A hawk inspired English poet John Skelton when he sought a creature to match the character of his beloved.

> *Merry Margaret,*
> *As midsummer flower,*
> *Gentle as falcon*
> *Or hawk of the tower.*

Horses

"THERE is no secret so close as that between a rider and his horse," said the English sportsman Robert S. Surtees. Mutual trust and understanding seem to exist beyond definable limits and reach a realm of cosmic strangeness. The presence of such a mysterious rapport ranks one of nature's most splendid creations in a class by itself.

Wild horses, ancestors of the domestic animal, still graze on Mongolian plains in diminishing number as the ancient species approaches extinction. Conquest and commerce brought the horse westward where it evoked awe and delight, its place in myth and legend assured.

The Hyksos, an errant horde of Asiatic horsemen, invaded and conquered Egypt in the 17th century B. C. The introduction of the horse and war chariot to the land of the pharaohs brought humiliating defeat. Nonetheless, Egyptians were captivated by the quality and potential of the animal. Two hundred years passed before the Hyksos were expelled, but during that time Egyptians became proficient in breeding and tending horses. Empire builder Thutmose III, who ruled from 1479 to 1425 B. C., rejoiced over his son's passion for the animal: "Now when he was a lad, he loved his horses, he delighted in them, he was persevering at exercising them and knowing their ways, skilled in training them." The Pharaoh

ordered his retinue: "Let there be given to him the very best horses of the stable of his majesty which is in Memphis. Tell him to take care of them." Thutmose revealed a basic equestrian truth, for it is not enough to ride well. Devotion to care is essential in order to win the confidence of high-strung and sensitive creatures. Too late an arrival to garner religious significance, the horse was beloved and treasured for its uncanny awareness of the unseen.

The ancient Greeks were equally charmed by the horse. It has been said that the first sight of a horse and rider inspired the concept of the mythological centaur — half man and half horse. Myths credit Poseidon, god of the sea, with creation of the first horse during a contest with Athena. Zeus decreed that whichever deity created the most useful object to mankind should have the honor of naming a beautiful new city. Athena dreamed up the olive tree, won the contest, and named the site Athens. But it must be conceded that Poseidon's creation is more universally valuable. Many tales are told of the winged horse Pegasus, sired by Poseidon and born of Medusa, whose sacred duty was to carry thunder and lightning to Zeus on Mount Olympus.

The *ashvamedha* or horse sacrifice, a reflection of earlier Scythian horse offerings to the Sun, was a distinctive Indian ceremony from 1000 to 50 B. C. In Hindu lore the horse often represented Surya, the Sun god. Epona (Divine Horse) was worshipped in Gaul as goddess and protector of horses by Celtic tribes.

White horses were sacred symbols in the British Isles. A prehistoric hill figure known as the Uffington White Horse, some 360 feet in length, gallops across the Berkshire Downs. Cut into turf to expose the chalk beneath, the White Horse was for centuries scoured every seven years during an ancient festival of unknown origin. Some scholars connect the monument with Gaul's Epona. Others speculate that the White Horse is a tribute to the Welsh goddess Rhiannon. Odin, the dominant god of Scandinavian legend, rode the eight-legged steed Sleipnir, faster than the wind, on his visits to the land of the dead. Another Norse myth tells of Alsvidur, the all-swift horse, which drew the chariot of the Moon goddess.

Fleetness is but one of the qualities admired in the horse. Ancient people believed that the fastest mares were with foal from the winds. Folklore holds that horses possess clairvoyance, often refusing to proceed or shying mysteriously when no visible obstacles are in view. They are believed especially susceptible to the Evil Eye and in Italy are often adorned with brass amulets to avert the *jettatora*.

The horse owns a year in the Oriental zodiac. Its natives are deemed spirited, often possessing peculiar psychic power. Mystical themes regarding the horse are prevalent throughout the world. The wonderfully strange communication achieved between human and equine continues to be an elusive factor.

Peacocks

Peacock display   Zurich, 1560

BEAUTY is the keyword to define the magical peacock. A spectacular train of iridescent feathers — purple, blue-green, copper, gold and bronze — is the pride of the adult male bird. The glory of his train fanned out in courting display excites the peahen, assuring the continuation of the species. And it is the shimmering beauty of peacock plumage that has always attracted human admiration.

Native to India, the peacock attained divinity in Hinduism, for its qualities symbolized Indra, god of thunder, rain, and war. Reasons for the association are evident. The peacock's courtship ritual includes an ear-splitting scream. Breeding season occurs just before India's summer monsoons, and the raucous cries herald rain. A fierce fighter and predator of snakes, the peafowls' powerful claws and iron beak equip them successfully to dispatch a cobra or other poisonous reptiles. Chosen as the Indian national bird in 1963, peacocks continue to enjoy the favored status conferred since Asoka, third-century B. C. emperor, decreed a limit on their slaughter. Peacock feathers are emblems of strength and good fortune throughout the East. In the West, a contrary theme developed.

The semi-tame bird has a sedentary nature and is content in captivity as long as food, water, and a comfortable environment are provided. Nobility of ancient kingdoms imported pairs to breed, and peacocks graced the gardens of Babylon, Egypt, Persia, and Greece. Alexander the Great so admired the bird that he imposed heavy fines on individuals hunting them as game. The Greeks associated peacocks with the goddess Hera, queen of heaven.

Hera's role in early Greek myth is singularly unpleasant. She was depicted as a beautiful woman, but proud, insanely jealous, vindictive, cold and cruel beyond measure. Her primary concern was to punish women with whom her husband Zeus dallied. One myth relates that Zeus transformed his lover Io into a white heifer to allay Hera's suspicion. But she, accustomed to his trickery, demanded the cow as a gift. The guilty Zeus agreed. When Hera set Argus of One Hundred Eyes to guard the creature, Zeus sent his clever son Hermes to retrieve Io. Hermes lulled all One Hundred Eyes to sleep with music, slew Argus and set the heifer free. When she discovered the crime, Hera gathered up the eyes of Argus and in a towering rage flung them over the long train of her peacock — ever to serve as a reminder of the treachery.

Another characteristic of Hera was vanity. A peacock's first priority upon waking is to fastidiously preen its feathers. A notable passage in Homer's *Iliad* describes Hera grooming herself to seduce Zeus, whose love for her had grown cold. Her success changed the course of the Trojan War.

The reputation of the peacock suffered as a result of its identification with Hera. The "eyes" of its plumage came to symbolize the Evil Eye. Many Western occult traditions regard peacocks as omens of ill fortune and their feathers as tokens of bad luck.

But perhaps beauty alone is reason enough to cherish the bird. In a sixth-century B.C. fable of Aesop, the peacock complains to Hera that while the nightingale pleases every ear with its song, a peacock's cry is met with laughter. The goddess consoles him, "But you far excel in beauty and size. The splendor of the emerald shines in your neck, and you unfold a tail gorgeous with painted plumage." Her answer fails to satisfy the peacock and he asks, "But for what purpose have I this dumb beauty so long as I am surpassed in song?" Hera explains that the lot of each bird is assigned by the will of the Fates: "To thee, beauty; to the eagle, strength; to the nightingale, song; to the raven, favorable, and to the crow, unfavorable, auguries. Be content with your lot; one cannot be first in everything."

Roosters

APHRODITE, goddess of love, and Ares, god of war, engaged in an illicit love affair. To be sure that their meetings were kept secret, a youth named Alectryon promised to keep watch and give warning should anyone approach. Unfortunately, Alectryon fell asleep. The Sun rose, spied the lovers, and reported the adultery to Hephaestus, Aphrodite's husband. Since he was the god of metal-working, Hephaestus took revenge for the affront by forging a wondrously fine net and casting it over the guilty pair. Aphrodite and Ares, unable to escape, were exposed to the delight and ridicule of their fellow Olympians. When finally released, a furious Ares transformed Alectryon into a rooster and banished him to the barnyard, decreeing that ever after he must crow at sunrise. From this myth, recounted by Homer in the *Odyssey*, came the Greek word *alektryon*, cock, and the bird's role as herald of dawn.

The cock is ruler of a large harem of hens, noted for his feisty spirit, and his destiny is intertwined with love and war. Anyone who has gathered eggs from a hencoop can testify to a rooster's aggressive nature. Ancient warriors of the Middle East wore helmets adorned with a crest that has been likened to a cockscomb, and similar gear was displayed down to Roman times. Such a headpiece might imbue a soldier with the bird's courage and pugnacity. Cockfighting, a bloody battle to the death, was an early form of entertainment and still has its adherents.

When the sun rose and dispelled darkness, human spirits were lifted. Dawn, some say, is the enemy of evil. When it became the cock's crow that pronounced the end of night, the bird himself was regarded as a solar symbol. His image appeared on coins, amulets, and weathervanes. Helios and Apollo, Greek gods of the Sun, and the goddess Persephone, personification of rebirth and springtime, received the cock as an emblem. Depictions of the bird are absent from the tombs and temples of ancient Egypt because the fowl was not introduced in that land until 1400 B. C. The Romans dedicated the rooster to Mercury in his role as god of commerce. At the turn of the Common Era, the Gnostic sects of Alexandria portrayed their Sun god Abraxas with a cock's head.

The rooster is an Oriental bird. Its common ancestor is the Red or Indian Junglefowl, *Gallus ferrugineus*, native to southern Asia. We might expect the bird to hold sacred significance in the East, where he rules a year of the Chinese lunar calendar. As one of the twelve creatures to whom Buddha granted the power to bestow its own characteristics upon those born in its time span, the cock year gives its natives flamboyance, self-assurance, an aggressive nature, and a devotion to minutia. A Ming Dynasty sculpture of *feng-huang*, a magical bird of Chinese legend, bears a strong resemblance to the rooster. As the most exalted of the four spiritual creatures — tortoise, unicorn, dragon — *feng-huang* only appeared in times of peace and prosperity.

Sheep

ON A STEEP cliff wall in Algeria where the Sahara Desert meets the Atlas Mountains is a remarkable engraving made over seven thousand years ago. An enormous ram towers over a man whose arms are raised as if in awe. The ram wears a decorative neck band and is crowned with a large disk from which rays emanate. This area was once fertile land where herds of wild sheep grazed and the ram commanded interest and respect.

The image portends the sanctity the ram would eventually hold farther east in the Nile Valley. In ancient Egypt's predynastic times Khnemu, a god associated with creation, was portrayed as a ram or a ram-headed man crowned with the solar disk. The great god Amon, whose worship combined with the power of the Sun god, Ra, claimed the ram as his symbolic creature. The massive complex of ruins at Karnak includes a magnificent avenue of ram-headed sphinxes leading to the Great Temple of Amon-Ra. God of gods, Amon-Ra signified a mysterious hidden force that created and sustained the universe. Greek and Roman visitors would equate Amon-Ra with their chief god Zeus/Jupiter.

The Roman astrologer and poet Manilius credits the Egyptian priesthood with the development and refinement of astrology. And it may be due to the prestige of Amon-Ra that Aries the Ram is the first sign of the zodiac. "Resplendent in

his golden fleece the Ram leads the way," wrote Manilius around the turn of the Common Era. The "golden fleece" refers to the ram of Greek myth that saves two children from death and is then sacrificed to the gods, his fleece later becoming the prize sought by Jason and the Argonaut expedition. The astrological personality assigned to the Ram in the West is bold and audacious. The Sheep of Oriental astrology displays far different characteristics. Natives of a Sheep Year are gentle souls, never forceful or dynamic.

Sheep were among the world's earliest domesticated animals, and their contrary gender images — strong male and meek female — surfaced in various cultures down the ages. The Hebrews honored the male's power in wartime and in religious ritual. The shofar, a ram's horn, was once used for its blare to issue battle signals, and is still to be heard in synagogues over the High Holidays. Christianity favored the more serene sheep, and the themes of the shepherd and his flock, the purity and innocence of the lamb, appear often in church doctrine. In the Roman Catholic Church, bishops carry the crosier, or shepherd's crook, as an emblem of their pastoral duty toward their human flocks.

Swine

THE MAGICAL history of the pig is paradoxical, sometimes receiving its due as an excellent creature, sometimes reviled. Through the ages the wild boar was universally renowned for courage and intelligence. Domestication occurred first in China, where the pig was accorded respect. Representing a year in the Oriental astrological cycle, a boar native would be indolent, honest, generous, and a seeker of harmony. Buddhist lore pronounces the pig lazy and vulnerable to attack, but pig talismans are often used in the Orient and India to ward off angry demons. Another porcine image appears in the Hindu creation myth relating how Vishnu, incarnated as the boar Varaha, raises the earth goddess from the primeval sea.

The pig's fate swung from divine to abominable when Semitic tribes of the Levant herded swine. Hebrews were forbidden to kill or eat pigs, a dictum interpreted by some scholars as evidence that the animals were originally considered sacred. A biblical admonition to refrain from casting pearls before swine clearly indicates a marked aversion to the animal. Arabs shared the same attitude, for the Koran prohibits eating pork. Some historians suggest that since pork becomes rancid without refrigeration in hot climates, the religious dietary laws merely reflect an awareness of the danger. But even in Egypt where most animals were revered, a piglike creature portrayed the evil god Set — he who cut the grain Osiris planted. Pork was traditionally eaten only once a year at the Midwinter Feast, and those who tended swine were considered unfit to enter the temples of the gods. The theme that pigs are unclean prevailed throughout the Middle East despite the fact that the animals are by nature fastidious.

The pig's fortune improved in Greece, for it was deemed sacred to Demeter, goddess of vegetation. And although the wild boar was notorious for ravaging crops, it was credited as well with teaching farmers to churn up the earth. Greek myths associate the pig with purity and protection from evil spirits.

Apollo purifies Orestes   Greek, 5th century B.C.

Apollo raised a pig above the head of Orestes to absolve him of guilt for the death of his mother. Initiates to the Eleusinian Mysteries, the highest spiritual rite of ancient Greece, used the pig in liturgy. They took charge of a young pig and ceremonially washed both pig and themselves in the sea on the journey from Athens to Eleusis, where they would comprehend Demeter's mystic truths. According to Homer, the fair-haired sorceress Circe was so offended by the ill manners of Odysseus' ravenous crew that she transformed them into swine. The colorful fiction lives on to give pigs an undeserved reputation for greed.

Pigs fared better in northern Europe. Scandinavian legends honored the boar as a formidable enemy. Warriors carried shields emblazoned with a boar's head as a protective emblem. Nordic tribes, hoping to be imbued with the animal's valor, feasted on roast pork. A magnificent golden boar named Gollinborsti (Goldenbristles) belonged to the Norse deities Freyr and Freya. The Celts especially sensed the animal's otherworldly qualities. Supernatural boars and magical pigs abound in their myths. The Welsh tale of Twrch Trwyth, a king transformed into a great boar, is a notable example. King Arthur and his men hunted the beast for the mysterious treasure he held between his ears.

Nuggets of ancient wisdom survive in folklore and rural customs. Pigs are believed to understand the voice of the wind and can predict the weather. Porcine intelligence and response to music confounds some people with fear of devil possession. A persistent motif contends that the words "pork" and "bacon" must not be mentioned within the hearing of swine. Wise farmers pay heed.

WILD CREATURES

We share the planet with thinking animals.   Each species, with its uniquely sculpted mind, endowed by nature and shaped by evolution, is capable of meeting the most fundamental challenges that the physical and psychological world presents.   Although the human mind leaves a characteristically different imprint on the planet, we are certainly not alone in this process.

— MARC D. HAUSER

Bats

IN THE PERFECT system that is the natural world, bats are perhaps the most vilified. They are virtuous little creatures that provide us with a variety of enormous benefits. Without bats on the job, we would be shrouded in insects. Worldwide, bats are the most voracious destroyers of flying pests, able to gobble as many as six hundred mosquitoes in an hour. In Texas the furry flyers repay hospitality by wiping out about twenty thousand tons of insects a year. Farmers in the South-west and in tropical climates, where cacti and other plants flower at night, welcome bats for the sexual courier service of moving pollen from blossom to blossom.

But misconceptions are rife. Neither birds nor rodents, bats are members of the order *Chiroptera*, "hand wing," the only mammals to have evolved true flight. Their sheer numbers are stunning; nearly one thousand species account for about one quarter of all mammals.

At night bats emerge from their sunless sleeping quarters, caves or dark spaces in buildings, and flap out to feed. They scare people by flying with mouths agape and little teeth glistening, a sight that in no way signifies aggression. The creatures are squeaking to "see" by echolocation. Similar to sonar, the method works so beautifully that bats can evade a thread strung in the pitch dark, which puts to rest another eerie fallacy — that bats fumble their way into women's hair. Amanda Lollar, author of *The Bat in My Pocket*, is enchanted by bats. Lollar met her first as she gingerly tended the injured creature and became charmed with the bat's quirky character. The author discovered that her "troll doll" had an irresistibly mischievous, loving personality and surpassed dogs and cats in intelligence. "She had a reaction to everything," Lollar wrote, "excitement, boredom, happiness, hunger or affection. All of them could be read on her face, and her chitterings took on different notes to match these emotions."

Historical records show a dearth of bat pets, but conflicting beliefs do turn up in ancient cultures. The Chinese believed that bats were lucky, and further maintained that they flew head downwards to accommodate the weight of their brains. Some Africans considered bats sacred, embodying the souls of the dead. Native Americans used them in initiation rituals, symbolizing rebirth as creatures emerging from the dark cave of Mother Earth's womb.

But bats have long had mysterious and terrifying associations. To the Irish the bat is a death symbol, and a flying phantom to the aborigines of British Columbia. In most of the world the entry of a bat into a house portends the death of an occupant. In medieval times people believed that the Devil assumed the shape of a bat, entered the human body, and only exorcism could rid the victim of the fluttering monstrosity.

Which brings us to vampire bats. An obscure species of tiny toothless South American bats does seek the blood of cattle and small mammals, but has no taste for the human neck. The foundation of today's vampire craze began with the publication of Bram Stoker's *Dracula*, which itself never stressed the bat connection. The mischief has been cinematic. In 1922 the eerie legend turned up in the German Expressionist film *Nosferatu, A Symphony of Horror*, followed nine years later by the Bela Lugosi *Dracula*, a runaway hit, with the undead's black cape morphing into bat wings. Since then there have been many films with bats featured as purveyors of terror — and reinforcing the dark beliefs.

Butterflies

THE CHILEAN poet Neruda calls them "flying violets," a child friend calls them "flutterbys." Whatever the terminology, our hearts lift at the sight of a butterfly, the essence of beauty and freedom. The Greek word "psyche" means both "soul" and "butterfly," and since ancient times the elegant airborne creature has symbolized rebirth. Its own life cycle is a dazzling metamorphosis. The butterfly begins as a caterpillar and transforms into a pupa enclosed in a cocoon. Inside the form-fitting home it modifies, struggles out, shakily unfolds itself and flies off with the simultaneous wings rippling. Nourishment is simplicity itself, requiring only nectar. Milkweed, verbena and red clover delight the butterfly, which alights on the flower and uncoils its long tongue to sip the refreshment. The gorgeous creature will live only a month, a short but blithe life.

To the imaginative Greeks the soul took two butterfly forms. In its earliest image the soul was depicted as a tiny person with butterfly wings like a fairy; later a butterfly itself signified the soul. An uncanny similarity of the butterfly/spirit link exists in almost as many places as clouds of butterflies bless with their presence. Some Germans believe that the dead are reborn as children who fly as butterflies. In Assam, Nagas assert that death brings a number of transformations in the underworld, ending with rebirth as a butterfly. The dying man chooses his form of rebirth in the Solomon Islands, and butterflies are the favored choice. And in sites as scattered as Cornwall, Siberia and Mexico, white butterflies inspired the most awe as repositories of dead souls. But Finns and others believe that the butterfly-soul can vacate the body while a person sleeps, accounting for dreams. And the Serbs have unique associations with sleep, butterflies and witchcraft. If they can find a sleeping witch and turn the body around without waking her, the soul will be unable to find the mouth for reentering its abode and the witch will die.

Butterflies also flutter their way into some creation myths. A Sumatran tribe claims descent from three brothers hatched from butterfly eggs, although they married heavenly wives sent down fully grown. Legends of the Pima tribe of Arizona declare that Chiowotmahki, the Creator, transformed itself into a butterfly and flew over the world until it found the optimum place for mankind.

Similarity also exists in a few places where people believe butterflies are taboo. Their cousins the moths are widely regarded as malicious witch spirits, and sometimes the disfavor extends to butterflies. In medieval Westphalia, St. Peter's Day featured a tradition of butterfly banishment. Children ran around the villages knocking on houses with hammers and reciting incantations to drive the creatures outside. Perhaps the reason for this obviously mock ritual is the ancient belief that butterflies steal the butter.

Capture is viewed as bringing luck in some places, usually with a brief ritual. In the German town of Oldenburg, the first butterfly of the season should be caught and flown through your coat sleeve. If you spot the first white of the season in Essex, England, tradition directs you to bite off its head but allow it to fly away. It's our guess that many a blind eye must be turned toward the first white butterfly. Folks in Suffolk tell us that you must "tenderly entreat" the resplendent captive. Nice idea. Next time you find one of the beauties, watch it for a moment, wish it a blissful nectar-filled life, and voice your own hope for the same.

Crows and Ravens

YOU PROBABLY never have pondered until you were weak and weary about the nature of ravens and crows, but these seemingly ordinary creatures have an amazing mythology. Sometimes the raven, *Corvus corax*, is singled out, sometimes the crow, *Corvus brachyrhynchos*. The stories vary from their guises as creators of the world to sinister forces to oracles, especially in deciding the fate of soldiers in combat. The birds also feature in a flock of accounts as raucous practical jokers, perhaps derived from their actual playful natures. Crows and ravens enjoy chasing each other in sky acrobatics and have been known to buzz dogs, cats and sometimes people, apparently whooping it up just for fun.

From Siberia to North America, Crow and his big brother Raven star in an ancient cycle of creation myths. The Haida of the Queen Charlotte Islands, for instance, believed that a huge Raven created mankind. At first Raven flew alone, but solo flight became lonely and he wanted companions. He spotted a clam shell on the shore and spit on it. By and by he heard voices from the shell, pried it open with his beak, and freed the first human beings. In many genesis stories Raven imparted his own greedy, irreverent spirit to all he touched. Legend has it that as a final joke he added genitals to the creatures he made, "Raven's greatest game."

In some tales the sooty bird originates as a beautiful white bird, an attendant on gods and heroes. Such a crow, white as milk, served as Apollo's oracular bird. When the god fell in love with the mortal Coronis, he suspected that she was unfaithful and commanded the crow to spy her out. When the bird flew back with a report of her dalliance with Ischys, Apollo was enraged at the messenger as well as the lovers. Since the bird had failed to blind Ischys with its sharp beak, as crows were believed to do when irked with humans, Apollo turned the crow black — from ancient times the color of death and disaster.

A tale from Native Americans also accounts for transformation to the dusky color. The Raven-Who-Sets-Things-Right was a pure white bird who reclaimed the earth from wasteland to paradise for the first humans. The Old One, a rich miser who lived at the end of the earth, hoarded the fresh water, food and fire. Raven stole the elements and from them created mountains, forests, rivers and streams, stocking them with animals and fish. And to enhance the human condition further and deliver man from bleak darkness, he stole the Old One's bag of moon and stars and flung them into the sky. But during one of the burglaries, he was caught in the smoke hole of the tent and hung helpless until his gleaming white feathers were coated with an everlasting sootiness.

An elaborate mythology about the birds wove its way into Celtic and Norse lore, often as superb battlefield magic. Early Danes fought under a pure white banner until the heat of battle, when a raven would appear on the flag; its wings drooped if the Danes were doomed, spread wide to presage victory. Mighty Odin himself kept company with two ravens, Thought and Memory, one perched at each shoulder. At first light they flew into the world, swiftly circling the globe in opposite directions and checking out the follies of mankind. When they returned to Valhalla, the ravens croaked the news of the day into the god's ears. The Morrigan, "Great Queen," is the Celtic goddess of battle and fertility. In old, old stories she turns up either as a single entity or as a trio with Badb and Macha, all of whom hover over the combat in the guise of crows cawing incantations. Perhaps one was "nevermore," the most unlucky word Poe could imagine. But in the epic *Beowulf*, the black bird heralds sunrise.

> *The black-coated raven,*
> *Blithesome of spirit,*
> *Hailed the coming of Heaven's bliss.*
> *Then over the shadows uprose the sun.*

In tales menacing or benevolent, crows and ravens are never depicted as bird brained; much mythology reflects their very real intelligence. "If men had wings and bore black feathers, few of them would be clever enough to be crows," declared the 19th-century theologian Henry Ward Beecher. The ultimate cleverness of crows is reflected in Aesop's famous fable: "A thirsty crow found a pitcher with some water in it, but so little was there that, try as she might, she could not reach it with her beak, and it seemed as though she would die of thirst within sight of the remedy. At last she hit upon a clever plan. She began dropping pebbles into the pitcher and with each pebble the water rose a little higher until at last it reached the brim, and the bird was enabled to quench her thirst." That was one smart crow, but one could expect nothing less from a Corvid.

Aesop's Fables   Arthur Rackham, 1912

Deer

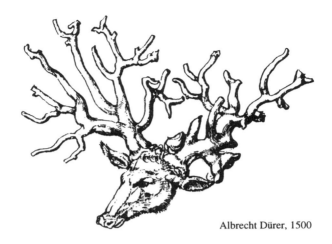

Albrecht Dürer, 1500

ELEGANT, swift, shy and elusive describe one of the world's most beautiful animals. Thirty-four species of deer have adapted to environments from arctic to tropic in North and South America, Europe, northwest Africa and Asia. Wherever deer exist, people have told mystical tales about them.

The earliest hint of their otherworldly nature is a striking rock painting known as the Sorcerer, c. 12,000 B.C. Deep in the cavern of Les Trois Frères in southern France a human figure wearing antlers dominates a wall covered with engravings of myriad animals. The stag and his antlers, both widely regarded as supernatural, have ever been associated with shamans and many forms of pagan worship.

The theme of transformation constantly occurs in deer legend and folklore. The Greek goddess of the hunt, Artemis, favored deer above all creatures and displayed a cruel streak when she took revenge on a hapless hunter. Actaeon's only sin was to accidentally glimpse the goddess and her nymphs bathing in a mountain pool. Artemis was so offended at being observed naked by a mere mortal that she sprayed Actaeon

Artemis   Ernst Lehner, 1912

with water which turned him into a stag doomed to be killed by his own hounds.

An old English legend with deer and metamorphosis as the primary motif concerns Lady Sybil of Bernshaw Tower in Lancashire. She was beautiful, wealthy, "intellectual beyond most of her sex," and irresistibly drawn to the practice of witchcraft, for which she showed remarkable talent. Lady Sybil loved nature with all her heart and enjoyed nothing so much as to ramble through the deep ravines of Cliviger Gorge in the form of a milk-white doe. One May Eve in this guise she was captured by Lord William of Townley Castle with the magical help of another Lancashire witch, the famous Mother Helston.

It all began in early spring a very long time ago. Lord William had nearly despaired of ever winning the lovely heiress of Bernshaw Tower as his bride. She was indifferent to his courting and repeatedly spurned his advances. But Mother Helston prepared a powerful spell woven into a long silken chord and loaned Lord William her own familiar, a fierce black hound. With these the nobleman won his heart's desire, for at cock's crow the captive doe became Lady Sybil, now docile and subject to his will. But Lord William made a fatal mistake when he offended Mother Helston by failing to properly thank her for her efforts on his behalf.

Within one passage of the Moon the spell was lifted and Lady Sybil sought her freedom. Lord William was forced to hold her prisoner under the constant guard of his manservant Robin. One night while Robin dozed a splendid white cat tried to slip by him. Robin woke with a roar and with his dagger struck off the cat's paw. When he stooped to pick it up, in its place lay the severed hand of Lady Sybil, identified by an elaborate diamond ring on her forefinger. The hand was returned to its owner and magically restored to Lady Sybil's arm, although a faint red line remained. Lord William tried his best to make amends, but it was too late. The lady's health declined after this episode and she soon died.

According to her wishes, Lady Sybil was buried in Cliviger Gorge close by Eagle Crag, where as the white doe she had been run to ground by Mother Helston's hound. And when darkness falls on May Eve, so the legend tells, doe and hound and ardent hunter return to haunt the night.

Dolphins

PEOPLE tend to take dolphins into their hearts and the affection seems requited, for of all wild creatures these are especially enticed by our voices and music. Sailors rejoice in the sight of dolphins crashing through the waves and submerging like sleek little submarines, the swiftest of sea travelers. They plunge along at speeds of up to eighteen miles an hour, bottle noses cleaving the water, ever seeming to smile. Their intelligence is notable, and they clamor in complex whistles, clicks and clacks that madden scientists aspiring to break the language barrier.

The felicitous creatures have been committing random acts of kindness to humankind since antiquity. Old tales abound of dolphins rescuing swimmers, allowing children to ride their backs, herding schools of fish toward nets. Dolphins could even be summoned, the Roman historian Pliny tells us — when certain fishermen would shout *simo*, "snub nosed," dolphins often emerged as fishing companions and helpers.

Greek and Roman mythology is awash in dolphin tales. In one story Dionysus, the god of wine, hires a ship to cross the sea. Unaware of his identity, the crew plot to capture him and sell him into slavery. When Dionysus discovers the scheme, he manifests by flooding the ship with wine, sounding shrieking music like gale winds, turning the oars into snakes and the mast into a tangle of grapevines. The terrified sailors leap into the sea, where Poseidon transforms them into dolphins.

The creatures are associated with love and beauty — Eros and Aphrodite are often depicted riding dolphins. But the most potent legend associates dolphins with divine wisdom in their bond with Apollo, god of sunlight, music and the sacred mysteries of Delphi. On that site, originally called Pytho, a monstrous beast guarded a prophetess who inhaled trance-inducing vapors from a spring. When the Python arose from his lair beside the sanctuary, he lumbered out to terrorize the countryside, killing villagers and destroying crops. Apollo "killed the fearsome dragon Python, piercing it with his darts," as Homer tells us. But the monster was the son of the goddess Gaia, and as punishment for the kill Apollo was compelled to serve seven years as a cowherd in a distant land. When he wished to return, the deity assumed the guise of a dolphin, leaped aboard a Cretan ship and received passage. The site was renamed Delphi in honor of the dolphin, *delphis*, and Apollo took possession of the spring. Now often termed Apollo Delphinius, he bestowed divine powers on its priest-ess, who chewed laurel leaves as she muttered ambiguous oracles. Delphi, the prime Apollonian cult site, became the most powerful oracular center of the ancient world.

The dolphin also has a Poseidon connection. The lusty deity with the roving eye wished to possess the nereid Amphitrite. But she distrusted the sea god, known to play unattractive practical jokes with squid, jellyfish and octopus. Amphitrite fled to the mountains, but her persistent lover sent numerous messengers pleading his amorous cause. Finally, curiously enough, it was a beguiling dolphin that won her heart for Poseidon and Amphitrite returned to the underwater realm as queen of the sea. The grateful god thrust the dolphin into the heavens, eternally surging as the constellation Delphinus.

As above, so below, for we have miniature versions of the marvelous creatures in our own gardens. Some poetic horti-culturist noticed that the nectar cups of a plant resembled tiny dolphins leaping up the spike, and so named the lovely ruffled flower delphinium.

Frogs and Toads

FROGS and toads share a similar mythology, often negative, but toads fare even worse than frogs. Perhaps that is because frogs appear slightly more attractive to the human eye. Both are anurans, often aquatic, both have protruding eyes, webbed feet and large mouths, but frogs have smooth skins while toads tend to have squat, warty bodies. Frogs leap; toads flop along hop by awkward hop.

Down the ages frogs have inspired both repugnance and reverence. You might remember the fairy tale princess who kissed the frog and poof! A prince appeared. But in the original Grimm Brothers tale no kiss took place; the princess was revolted by the clammy croaker. She "flung him with all her might against the wall," and only then he became "a handsome prince with kind and grateful eyes."

Where frogs have aroused worship the watery creatures have been associated with rain, fertility and rebirth. Frog amulets have turned up in Egyptian tombs since the earliest dynasties, images of the goddess Heqet. Sometimes she was depicted as a frog, sometimes as a frog-headed woman, but always as "the Great Magician." Heqet represented the embryonic grain that seems to die, but then sends forth roots and sprouts. She lent her fertile presence when Isis had magical sexual union with the dead Osiris, god of resurrection, and Heqet presided as midwife when god of the rising sun, Horus, was born of the outlandish coitus. In fact Heqet gave all Egyptians life, they believed, for at the original creation she touched lifeless humans with the ankh, breath filled their lungs and movement began. Like other birth goddesses she was a prophet, perhaps because the croaking of a frog was held to predict rain and the life-enhancing rising of the Nile.

The ancient Jews, on the other hand, abhorred frogs. In the book of Revelation, seven angels "pour out on the earth the seven bowls of the wrath of God." The sixth bowl contained "three foul spirits like frogs," demonic forces "performing signs." And in Exodus the creatures were summoned by Moses to effect the second plague of Egypt.

Frog beliefs leap from demonology to healing. In the classical Greek/Roman world a person suffering from infection of the left or right eye would hang the corresponding frog's eye around his neck for a cure. For toothache, the Greek physician Galen had the patient hold in his mouth a frog boiled in vinegar and water. A later Roman physician believed toothache could be cured by spitting in a frog's mouth and asking it to take the pain away.

The aquatic creatures often connect to the deluge myths found everywhere. In Australia the aborigines say that a vast frog once drank all the water in the world and caused great drought and misery. If they could only make the frog laugh, they reasoned, he would expel the water. Several of the animals cavorted about acting silly, but the unamused frog kept his huge mouth clamped. Then an eel wriggled in a giddy dance. The frog roared with laughter, and the water poured forth again to refresh the earth and restore life.

Early in America, frog beliefs tended to create positive magic. People believed that good luck followed if a frog entered your house or if you dreamed of frogs. Gamblers would win if they encountered a frog on their way to gaming. And killing a frog would make your cow's milk bloody.

As for their cousins the toads, mostly landlubbers, people everywhere considered them nasty. Although a boon to the garden, the creatures had an evil image, partly based on the milky venom they exude from their skin when excited or irritated. Toads often served as witches' familiars, and in some parts of Europe were believed to be witches themselves. Old conjuring books mention a potion of "toad milk and the sap of sow thistle" for nefarious purposes. The deadly substance secreted in toads' glands is identified by modern science as a powerful hallucinogen named "bufotenin" for the toad family.

A medieval legend about an "old and great toad" that bore a gemstone in its head inspired Renaissance jewelers. At a time when poisoning one's enemies was rampant, a so-called "toadstone" ring was prized as a forewarning. The gem was often an emerald or green agate reputed to be so sensitive as to lose its natural color in the presence of poison. Amber, coral, or ivory were other choices said to produce a warning heat when in contact with venom. Trust in the ring sprang from the assumption that since the toad carried poison, it also carried a means within itself to detect and counteract the effects. In *As You Like It* Shakespeare writes:

> *Sweet are the uses of adversity,*
> *Which, like the toad, ugly and venomous,*
> *Wears yet a precious jewel in his head.*

Hares and Rabbits

I shall go into a hare
With sorrow and sighing and mickle care,
And I shall go in the Devil's name
Till I come home again.

WITH THIS verse Isobell Gowdie revealed a shape-shifting secret in freely given testimony during her trial for witchcraft in 1662. The young Scottish witch regaled the court for four days with tales of her mystic adventures. A widely accepted view at the time was that a witch could by incantation actually become an animal. The hare along with cat and crow, magical creatures all, were favored forms of transformation. The belief that a witch while in the shape of a rabbit could only be killed by a silver bullet became part and parcel of British folklore.

Distinctions are few between hare and rabbit. Hares are larger and wilder than their rabbit kin, and the rabbit is more inclined to accept domestication. In lore and legend, however, the two are interchangeable. Both animals are prolific and flourish worldwide. In many cultures, past and present, hares and rabbits serve as fertility symbols.

Hares lead hounds and hunters a merry chase, swift when pursued and a marvel in zigzag coursing. Classical myths align the hare with fleet-of-foot Hermes, the messenger god and guide of the dead. An antique fable claims that Hermes placed the constellation Lepus, the Hare, in the heavens just out of range of Orion to annoy the mighty hunter.

Julius Caesar observed that Gauls held the hare sacred, and

to hunt the animal or eat its flesh was forbidden. The ban was lifted only once a year on May Eve. The penalty for hunting hare at other times was to be struck with cowardice. The legendary British queen Boadicea, while leading a revolt against Roman rule, carried a hare into battle. She released it at a crucial moment in hope that the Romans would strike at it with their swords and thus lose courage. The taboo about eating rabbit persisted for centuries, due to fear that the animal's timid nature might be consumed as well.

In medieval Europe hares and rabbits acquired a reputation for mystery and magic. Their movements divined future events, and the unexpected sight of a hare or rabbit foreshadowed disaster. These creatures were, after all, allies of Hermes, the master magician, and companions of pagan woodland goddesses. Among the forty species of hares and rabbits, most choose to graze at twilight or at night. Nocturnal activity and kinship with the Moon alarmed the clergy.

In the East, from India to China, the hare and the Moon have close ties. Hindus see the hare's image on the Full Moon. The Buddha rewarded the hare with a place on the Moon, for it is said the creature leaped into a fire to save the holy man from starvation. According to Chinese legend, the Lunar Hare resides on the Moon under an acacia tree, where he pounds sacred herbs in a mortar to create the magical elixir of life.

In its own quiet way, the beautiful gentle hare/rabbit attained magical status. Perhaps that is why Lewis Carroll's Alice found Wonderland by following a white rabbit.

Alice's Adventures in Wonderland　　　　　　　　Arthur Rackham, 1907

Owls

THE BEHAVIOR of owls evokes dread. Their weird, melancholy call in an almost human voice shatters the still of the night. It may be followed by a blood-curdling shriek or a sound resembling mirthless laughter. The owl, with hunting skill that rivals the hawk's, is a nocturnal bird of prey with extraordinary hearing and keen eyesight. Its soft plumage assures silent flight ending in a swift kill. Owls choose to live in dark forests, thick pine groves, and deserted ruins. You will never see a flock of owls, for these creatures prefer a solitary existence. Mobs of other birds, especially crows, are ever ready to attack owls. From time to time, owls must seek refuge in hollow trees, abandoned nests, or caves. If encountered by day an owl shows no fear and may appear tame to the human intruder. However, its watchful stare and cool manner implies equality. The meeting may awaken thoughts of lost souls damned to live on as creatures of darkness and evil.

Owls live in all parts of the world and sinister themes permeate their lore and myth. A compelling tale is found in *The Maginogion*, Welsh legends of the early Celtic world collected from oral tradition and written down in medieval times. Arianrod, mother of Llew, declared that her son should "never have a wife of the race that now inhabits this earth." Gwydion and Math, powerful magicians and protectors of Llew, were angered by Arianrod's prohibition and determined to thwart her will. By charms and illusion, they conjured a wife for Llew out of flowers. With blossoms of oak, broom, and meadowsweet, they produced a maiden, "the fairest and most graceful that man ever saw." They named her Blodeuwedd.

Llew and his bride prospered until one day in Llew's absence a young hunter appeared at Blodeuwedd's door. As soon as their eyes met, passion filled their hearts. Ardently declaring their love, the couple spent the evening rejoicing in its wonder. "Nor did they hesitate to embrace — and that night passed locked in each other's arms." The adulterous pair plotted to kill Llew. But Llew led a charmed life and could be slain only by a bizarre set of circumstances. Blodeuwedd, by deceitful means, secured the knowledge needed to do away with her husband, informed her lover, and arranged for the murder to take place. When Gwydion learned of Llew's fate, he vowed vengeance. Confronting Blodeuwedd, Gwydion said, "I will not slay thee, but I will do unto thee worse than that. For I will turn thee into a bird; and because of the shame thou hast done unto Llew, thou shalt never show thy face in the light of day henceforth; and that through fear of all other birds. For it shall be their nature to attack thee, and to chase thee wheresoever they may find thee."

On a cheerier note: ancient Egyptians designed a beautifully stylized owl, the hieroglyph representing the prepositions *in, from, of, at* — which explains the owl's frequent appearance on tomb and temple walls. The Greeks, bless them, chose the owl as Athena's bird. The goddess of wisdom endowed the bird with her own noble aspects

Snakes

SNAKES inspire more fear than esteem, and the dread goes beyond the fear of venom — most snakes are harmless. Death by snakebite is a rarity in America, but that doesn't lessen the mortal terror many people experience at the sudden sight of a wriggling snake. Jung pointed out that the snake represents the underworld and primordial matter, a prototype of the dark unknown, primitive, earthly, sinister. And the prevailing serpent myth of the Judaic-Christian world, its role as tempter in the Garden of Eden, hardly adds to its charm.

Yet some people are drawn to snakes, fascinated by their subtle beauty, grace, and swift, sinuous movement. Snakes slither the earth garbed in shining geometric patterns, natural Art Deco creatures; Shakespeare refers to their "enamell'd skin." Perhaps the snake lovers among us, long ago and in another incarnation, belonged to a culture that revered these strange footless reptiles. To the ancient Greeks and Romans, the snake's habit of sloughing its skin symbolized renewal. Hermes/Mercury, the messenger god and spirit guide of the underworld, carried a snake-entwined staff, the caduceus. Asclepius, the god of medicine, was also associated with snakes, and the caduceus became the insignia of the medical profession. The sight of a serpent was an omen of healing to the ill, a certain promise of returning vigor.

The Gnostic sects in Alexandria around the turn of the Christian era chose a snake holding its tail in its mouth, the ouraboros, to depict the reconciliation of opposites. This Western version of the Oriental yin and yang, half in light and half in darkness, denotes the potent phrase *en to pan*, all is one.

Serpent worship turns up in a surprisingly wide variety of myths and legends. Ancient Egyptian deities and rulers are crowned with the sacred snake symbol, the uraeus. Voodoo venerates the serpent Damballah as the oldest and primary divinity, and snakes play a beneficent role from Australian aborigines to Native American tribes. The snake conspicuously slithered its way into Toltec, Aztec and Maya pantheons, emerging as the creator-god. They knew it as Quetzalcoatl, the plumed serpent, every coil covered in spectacular emerald-green feathers, god of wind, wisdom and life. Although the snake is often identified with underworld aspects, it is also associated with rainbows linking heaven and earth.

But despite such exalted roles elsewhere, for many people the glimpse of a curling snake evokes the same eerie feeling as Emily Dickinson voices:

> *Several of nature's people*
> *I know, and they know me;*
> *I feel for them a transport*
> *Of cordiality;*
>
> *But never met this fellow,*
> *Attended or alone,*
> *Without a tighter breathing,*
> *And zero at the bone.*

Spiders

THE SPIDER is commonly maligned. "Do you realize that if I didn't catch bugs and eat them, bugs would increase and multiply and get so numerous that they'd destroy the earth, wipe out everything?" The wise spider with the sweetly musical voice in E.B. White's *Charlotte's Web* is not just spinning a tale. She is ecologically correct. And when people spot one of her relatives in the house, what thanks do they generally offer? Brisk dispatch.

Several unsound reasons may exist for such antipathy. Humankind tends to feel uneasy about black creatures that move swiftly and silently. Spiders live alone, preferring solitude to the bustle of community life, and loners are often viewed with suspicion in our gregarious culture. Mostly we fear the bite of spiders, but these are seldom if ever fatal. The creatures do have one distressing trait by human standards; the male always dies after mating, sometimes from the bite of the female, sometimes from sheer exhaustion.

Spiders are not insects but with scorpions are classified as *Arachnida*, named for a great weaver in an ancient tale. Arachne was so proud of her work that she boasted it was more beautiful than the cloth Minerva wove. The goddess, who clothed in splendor all the deities on Mount Olympus, was outraged at the peasant girl's audacity and challenged her to a contest. Both set to their looms in Arachne's forest hut and their shuttles flew. According to the mythologist Edith Hamilton: " Minerva did her best and the result was a marvel, but Arachne's work, finished at the same moment, was in no way inferior. The goddess in a fury of anger slit the web from top to bottom and beat the girl around the head with her shuttle. Arachne, disgraced and mortified and furiously angry, hanged herself. Then a little repentance entered Minerva's heart. She lifted the body from the noose and sprinkled it with a magic liquid. Arachne was changed into a spider, and her skill in weaving was left to her."

As if to right a serious wrong toward spiders, many societies have held the spider to be lucky. The Greeks and Romans believed a spider engraved on a precious stone conferred foresight on one who wore it. According to Celtic lore, seeing a spider spinning is an omen that good fortune is near. And killing a spider in Britain was thought to bring on a long spell of rain. Confining a spider in a walnut shell to wear around the neck as a cure for ailments was as popular in the 18th century as when the ancient Greeks wore the same odd pendants.

Spiders are superb engineers. To watch a beautifully symmetrical web emerge from the hectic dance of the spider is fascinating — and in one historical instance inspiring. After a number of defeats against Britain, the Scottish liberator Robert the Bruce hid in a cave, vanquished and miserable. Looking up he sighted a spider attempting to anchor its web. Six times it failed, but the seventh try was successful. Taking such tenacity as a sign, the future king determined never to give up until he prevailed.

In 17th-century England Mirabel Bedford, an accused witch, kept a spider as a familiar and addressed it as Joan. Witches to this day hold a tender regard for the marvel of spiders and allow webs house room, holding to the old couplet:

If you wish to live and thrive, let a spider run alive.

Swans

SWANS belong to northern climes, the place viewed by ancient people as mysterious and magical. Breeding in the northernmost area of their range, swans wing south to winter in Europe, China, Japan, and the United States. Their great size and bright white plumage stirred the imagination. Swans gliding smoothly, silently on water were a sight of striking beauty and grace. The splendid visitors inspired myths for as long as there have been mythmakers.

A Native American legend of the Blackfoot tribe depicts swans as helpers in a hero's quest to visit the Sun. After a series of adventures, the youth faces a great expanse of water separating him from his goal. A hopeless feeling envelops him and then: "Two swans came swimming. They asked him who he was and what had brought him to that shore. He responded, and they said, 'Take heart. Across this water is the lodge of that Person Above whom you seek. Get on our backs, and we shall take you there.' He waded in, lay on their backs, and they started. Very deep and black is that water. Strange beings inhabit it: monsters that seize people and drown them. Yet the two swans carried him safely to the other shore, where a broad trail led from the water. 'Hyi!' said the swans. 'Follow that trail.'"

Another tale concerns transition and is the source of the expression "swan song" to describe a final performance. The story derives from Finland's ancient epic poem, the *Kalevala*.

Sibelius, the eminent Finnish composer, reflects the atmosphere of this runic legend in his hauntingly beautiful tone poem, "Swan of Tuonela." Tuonela, the land of death, is a dark underground kingdom ringed by a black river upon which a majestic swan glides. The swan's song is a plaintive melody, and whoever hears it must leave the reality of this world and venture into a strange, unknown land. The swan represents a spirit guide as the soul passes from one place to another.

Swan transformation myths are a recurrent theme in literature and other arts, from the tragic Irish tale, *Children of Lir*, to *Lohengrin*, the operatic Swan Knight of German lore, to the Russian tale of *Swan Lake*, basis of the lovely ballet.

Zeus, sky god of the Greeks, chose the guise of a swan in order to seduce Leda, queen of twilight. Their coupling produced two eggs. From the first came Castor and Pollux, the heavenly twins, and the second held Clytemnestra and the ill-fated Helen of Troy. Some scholars say Leda's spouse Tyndareus fathered one set of twins, but authorities differ over which egg was which. The myth inspired many painters, especially during the Renaissance, and most major museums possess a version of Leda and the Swan. The poet Yeats wrote a superb account of the seduction: "A sudden blow: the great wings beating still above the staggering girl..."

Apollo, Greek god of music and poetry, was linked to the bird, for it was believed that his soul passed into a swan. From this legend arose the tradition that the souls of all good poets live on as swans. Ben Jonson called Shakespeare the "Swan of Avon." Not only poets are affiliated with swans. Diogenes Laertius in his *Lives of Eminent Philosophers*, third century A.D., wrote: "Socrates in a dream saw a cygnet on his knees, which all at once put forth plumage, and flew away after uttering a loud sweet note. And the next day Plato was introduced as a pupil, and Socrates recognized him as the swan of his dream."

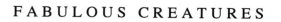

FABULOUS CREATURES

If there have been, are and always will be, more things in heaven and earth than were dreamed of in Horatio's philosophy, we must understand that one of the channels which led to the creation of fabulous animals was pure fact.

— T. H. WHITE

Basilisk

Basilisk
Nuremberg, 1510

BEWARE the basilisk unless, of course, you are carrying a weasel in a cage. Without such protection the beast can slay you in unpleasant ways. It is the Evil Eye made manifest, capable of "looking anyone dead." The range of the monster's fiery glance is so far-reaching that it can make a lark flying past plummet from the air, deliciously fried, into the gaping mouth. Where the monster roams becomes the bleakest of deserts. Nothing survives, for its visual venom blackens grass, rots the fruits of the earth and even splits rocks. Where the basilisk simply happens by, water turns toxic.

Sometimes called a cockatrice, the basilisk has the body of a large snake with the head and legs of a cock, wide thorny wings, and a tail ending in a hook or arrowpoint. Two stories prevail about the birth of the sinister creature. One tells us that it sprang from a round yolkless egg laid by a seven-year-old rooster and hatched by a toad. The other reveals that the

75

basilisk is the offspring of the Gorgon Medusa, whose glance turned living beings into stone and from whose jaws "snakes poured forth whizzing hisses with vibrating tongues, which, after the manner of a woman's hair flowing along the back, flapped about the very neck of the delighted Medusa. Upon her forehead turned towards you erect did serpents rise, and viper's venom flowed from her combed locks."

The basilisk's stare was so potent that a hunter raising a spear to the beast was slain as the poison flowed up the weapon and into the man's heart — also killing the horse upon which he was mounted.

The monster's name derives from the Greek term meaning "little king," for the ancients regarded the basilisk as the king of serpents. The creature's original aspect sprang from that of a cobralike snake, and over time the image of the crest on the head evolved into a cockscomb, perceived in legend as a crown. But through all its evolutions the basilisk's nature has always been considered dire, for snakes have had a bad press long before Genesis.

You may be wondering about the weasel. The ancient warning actually refers to the mongoose, a fierce little ferret notable in India for its aptitude in killing cobras. It performs the same service with basilisks, for on spotting a mongoose the basilisk turns its slithery tail and runs off. Should a mongoose not be handy when you encounter a basilisk, a mirror offers equal protection — if the creature sees its own image, it dies of fright.

In the 17th century, literal belief in the monster began to wane. The Spanish poet Quevedo wrote the beautifully logical, beautifully mocking lines about the basilisk: "If the man who saw you is still alive, / Your whole story is a lie, / Since if he has not died he cannot have seen you, / And if he has died, he cannot tell what he saw."

Centaurs

MAN from head to torso, horse from torso south, centaurs canter along in the retinue of Dionysus, celebrating the rites and delights of the vine with Pan, Silenus, Eros, satyrs, nymphs and bacchantes. Like other rural divinities centaurs are gross brutes, prone to lechery and drunkenness. They are the offspring of Ixion, a Greek mortal, and a cloud, yes, a cloud, begotten in this bizarre fashion: Hot-headed Ixion quarreled with his future father-in-law and killed him. Pursued for the murder, he prayed to Zeus for salvation so earnestly that the god granted him refuge on Mount Olympus. Ixion repaid the hospitality by attempting to seduce Hera, the wife of Zeus and queen of heaven itself. To test the ingrate's audacity, Zeus formed a cloud in the tempting shape of Hera, and Ixion promptly coupled with the beautiful goddess-who-wasn't-there. Further enraged, Zeus caused a monster to be born of the misty union. Centaurus, the beast created by the lust of Ixion and the malice of Zeus, mated with the mares of Thessaly and fathered the raunchy race of centaurs.

Enormously fond of horses, Greeks were unafraid of centaurs and relished their company in some tales. But on one notorious occasion their bestial behavior led to a full-scale battle. Invited to attend the wedding of the King of Thessaly, the carousing centaurs got so drunk that they attempted to ravish the women, including the bride. A brawl followed, with slaughter on both sides. Finally the centaurs galloped off, but returned later with allies armed with big rocks and uprooted pine trees. Despite the heavy rural artillery the centaurs were defeated, and the battle marked the last friendship between mankind and the centaurs.

The exception was Chiron, educated by Apollo and Artemis, granted wisdom and eternal life. He was the mentor of Greek heroes, including Achilles and Jason, each of whom served an apprenticeship in the wilderness with the centaur. And Chiron is also singular for ceding immortality. Accidentally shot with a magical poisoned arrow by his friend Heracles, the centaur preferred death to unending pain and passed his gift of everlasting life to the fire-giver Prometheus. Yet Chiron is still poetically eternal. Zeus thrust the image of the noble centaur into the heavens, where he may be seen wheeling the night skies as the constellation Sagittarius the Archer.

Chimera

Chimera   Etruscan bronze, 5th century B.C.

CHIMERA is another Greek mythological animal you don't want to chance meeting, not even in your dreams. The beast would be easy enough to recognize, having the head of a lion, the torso of a goat, and the tail of a serpent. Sometimes the chimera, a female, is depicted as having three heads — a snake's head springs from the tail and a goat's head springs from the body, in addition to the fierce frontal lion. To make the "mingled monster" even more unprepossessing, the chimera has a fiery breath that sizzles to a crisp anything within range except the odd hero. Homer tells us that "Her pitchy nostrils flaky flames expire;/Her gaping throat emits infernal fire."

The beast may have been a metaphor for her birthplace in Lycia, where a volcano is called the Chimera. Serpents pervade the base of the mountain, goats graze on the meadows above, and lions were rumored to lurk toward the arid top, which belched flames. Since lions do not actually inhabit Greece, and since no one had actually ever seen a chimera, at some point doubt began to arise as to the creature's actual existence. The skepticism led to the modern definition of a chimera, "a vain or foolish fancy."

But before disbelief more or less erased the chimera from zoology, a tale evolved of its slaying. The hero was Bellerophon, a young prince who had fallen under the spell of Philonoe, the princess of Lycia. Reluctant to part with his daughter, King Iobates dispatched Bellerophon to kill the chimera, certain that the unwelcome suitor would perish in flames. But the goddess Athena, inventor of the bridle and tamer of horses, took pity on the handsome prince. She presented him with a golden bridle and revealed how to capture milk-white Pegasus, winged steed of the gods. "He will help you win the battle," she promised.

At the fountain of Hippocrene, the prince threw the bridle over the horse's head and thrust the golden bit between his teeth. Immediately tamed by Athena's magic, the horse soared up with the mounted Bellerophon in search of the chimera. Guided by the stench of burning greenery, Pegasus swooped from the sky so swiftly and Bellerophon dealt such mighty blows that the monster finally lay lifeless, her power destroyed. In Lycia the deed was celebrated with much rejoicing and a royal wedding.

The tale enriches us with its whiff of the heroic — and with "chimerical," a useful word to evoke when we set off in hot pursuit of a foolish dream.

Dragons

OF ALL fabulous beasts, the dragon has found its way into the most legends. Everyone is familiar with the monster's image — a scaly serpentine body and tail, large batlike wings, stumpy legs with claws, glaring eyes, and a fang-rimmed mouth emitting flames and smoke. The creature's formidable appearance beautifully fits the archetype, for in Western mythology the dragon personifies wickedness. It is the antithesis of the hero, their battles the symbolic clash of good and evil.

The successful dragon-slayer risks his life but shines his way down through history. Similar stories abound. A dragon captures a beautiful virgin, usually royal, and usually binds her to a rock. A knight contends for her release, slays the monster and gets to wed the princess. St. George is perhaps the most notable dragon hero. In this tale from the Middle Ages, every year a maiden had to be sacrificed to prevent the beast from laying waste to the countryside. The year that the lot fell to the Princess Sabra, she was rescued by this dauntless champion of Christendom. St. George slew the beast with one blow of his magic sword Ascalon, and by the deed not only won the princess but won the town over to Christianity. In earlier Greek mythology the valiant Perseus fared the same with the same elements — the beautiful princess Andromeda chained to a cliff, a monster slain by a sword, an acclaimed hero, a wedding, an enduring romantic tale.

Early cultures had a literal belief in the existence of dragons, and the Romans had some odd ideas about their behavior. According to the historian Pliny, Ethiopian dragons in search of more hospitable climates often navigated the Red Sea to

St. George slays the dragon   Albrecht Dürer, 1505

Arabia. To make the crossing, four or five dragons coiled
together to form a boat, pumping their powerful legs, their
heads swaying above the water. Pliny also devotes a chapter
to remedies and benefits derived from slain dragons. He

assures us that their eyes, dried and stirred with honey, make a potion to prevent nightmares; that a litigant will win his case if dragon-heart fat is daubed on a gazelle hide and bound to the arm with sinews of a stag; dragon teeth, also tied to the body, assure the lenience of masters and the mercy of kings.

Despite its fiery breath, the dragon's mythological element is water rather than fire. It chooses to dwell in watery or misty caves, often as a guardian of treasure. In Teutonic mythology the dragon Fafnir lurks in a cave and keeps a hoard with occult powers. Siegfried slays the monster, the tale immortalized at stunning length in the Wagnerian operas.

But in the East, especially in China, people love dragons. A Dragon Year, which ushered in the new millennium, portends riches and harmony, and at New Year's vivid dragons are pranced through streets in Chinese communities all over the world. The creatures are believed to be the givers of laws, fertility, swords, painting and magic. In art, clouds issue from their mouths rather than fire. As beings of splendor dragons once flew on the nation's flag and are associated with the possessions of emperors: the dragon throne, the dragon boat, the dragon bed, and so on.

In the words of Jorge Luis Borges, "There is something in the dragon's image that fits man's imagination."

Griffins

THE GRIFFIN is a rarity, doubly royal. The creature has the head and wings of an eagle, king of birds, and the body of a lion, king of beasts; it is symbolically potent for dominion over earth and sky. Griffins are notable for their strength and intelligence, and an old text assures us that they are the size of eight lions and have the strength of one hundred eagles. A griffin can "bear to his nest flying a horse and a man upon his back or two oxen yoked together as they go at plow." The concept of mighty eagle-lions arose in the Middle East, and they often turn up in the art of the ancient Babylonians, Assyrians and Persians.

As befits royalty, griffins love anything that glitters, especially gold. They have the ability to sense buried treasure, and atop the trove they build nests of gold and lay eggs of agate. Many a missing jewel might have been found in the cache of a griffin high in a mountain aerie. They defend their riches against all possible plunderers, and griffins became notable as ferocious guardians of precious things, both their own and those of emperors and gods. The ancient Greeks believed that griffins, the duality both sun creatures, drew the golden chariot of the sun god Apollo across the sky each day. Alexander the Great yearned for his own griffin to fly him to the edge of the sky. Nemesis, goddess of retribution, held griffons sacred and sometimes called upon their services to enact revenge. But in its most noble portrayal, valiant and forbidding, the griffin emerged during the Middle Ages as a key figure in heraldry. It arises rampant on the coats of arms and banners of kings, generals, aristocrats — in "wakeful custody," balanced on one or two lion paws, ready to strike with talons. Fierce images of griffins often loom from Gothic churches as gargoyles, in earlier versions created to scare demons or avert evil, in later architecture mainly ornamental.

Griffins had no particular enmity for people, but they dispatched dragons, snakes and horses, although they sometimes mated with mares. Their progeny were hippogriffs, an odd assemblage of feathered flying horses.

The most famous griffin, superstar of the species, bumbles its delightful way through the pages of Lewis Carroll's *Alice in Wonderland.* A surrealistic punster, the Gryphon informs Alice that he studied with a classical master and learned Laughing and Grief.

"And how many hours a day did you do lessons?" asked Alice.

"Ten hours the first day; nine the next; and so on."

"What a curious plan!" exclaimed Alice.

"That's the reason they're called lessons," the Gryphon remarked, "because they lessen from day to day."

Gryphon fast asleep   Sir John Tenniel, 1865

Phoenix

Phoenix   Basle, 1557

MOST creatures spring from other creatures. But there is only one phoenix ranging the sky, and this rarest of birds clones itself everlastingly from the burned bones of its own body. When it has divided the air for five hundred years and its wings falter, the phoenix builds itself a nest atop an Arabian date palm tree. In this tree it collects cinnamon, spikenard and myrrh, and of those splendid materials builds a heap on which to enact its fiery perfumed death.

The nest of leaves and bark becomes both grave and cradle.

Here the bird flutters its wings so rapidly that sparks glitter among feathers, and in this way flames begin snapping from beak to claws. The dying bird sings so melodiously, so gloriously, that winged creatures throng from skies everywhere to marvel. The phoenix expires singing its incomparable dirge in a sphere of spicy sweetness.

A worm humps its way out of the ashes. From this smallness and smoothness a young phoenix emerges nine days later.

Some ancient myths tell us that the bird was crimson and gold and resembled an eagle; other legends claim that it was purple and resembled a heron; all agree that it was a creature of unsurpassed beauty.

Its first act is to pat together a little egg of its own charred remains mixed with myrrh. With the egg in its beak, the phoenix flies to Heliopolis, the City of Sun on the Nile Delta. It is accompanied by a throng of birds and more join in flight. And in Egypt, every five hundred years, the phoenix was welcomed by high ritual in the Temple of Atum-Ra. The bird deposited its father-self egg on the pyramidal summit of the sacred obelisk and swooped out to begin its cycle anew.

Alchemists chose the phoenix as their symbol and early chemists were located by the sign of the phoenix swinging above the door. The Old Testament mentions the bird in Job, and Christian monks who wrote medieval bestiaries took the phoenix as a point of departure for a scolding: "If the Phoenix has the power to die and rise again, why, silly man, are you scandalized at the word of God."

Beginning with the Renaissance and early scientific observation, the phoenix vanished from bestiaries. But the bird has never migrated from poetry. Since antiquity the phoenix has burned brightly in the hearts of poets, both as immortality symbol and as exotic legend. None wrote more beautifully about the bird than John Dryden:

So when the new-born Phoenix first is seen
Her feathered subjects all adore their queen,
And while she makes progress through the East,
From every grove her numerous train's increased;
Each poet of the air her glory sings,
And round him the pleased audience clap their wings.

Salamander

Salamander Frankfurt, 1687

THE ZOOLOGICAL salamander is an unremarkable little amphibian that resembles a lizard. But its mythological counterpart has a uniquely wondrous quality — a body so icy that it can withstand flames.

Numerous old stories attest to such sightings, including one by the Renaissance artist Cellini documented in his autobiography. At age five, gazing into a log fire, he spotted a little creature weaving its head, waving its tail and frolicking in the flames. Excitedly he called his father to witness the spectacle. The father, equally amazed, soundly smacked the boy's ear to assure that the child would remember the scene forever. The act was a deplorable memory aid, but Signor Cellini believed that they were seeing a sight granted few humans — a magical little dragon.

Belief concerning the salamander's marvelous virtue existed in ancient Egypt and Babylon. In Greece, Aristotle wrote that the salamander "not only walks through fire, but puts it out in doing so." Roman naturalist Pliny described the creature as "so intensely cold as to extinguish fire by its contact, in the same way that ice does." A medieval monk kept the myth alive by recording: "This animal is the only one which puts the flames out. Indeed, it lives in the middle of the blaze without being hurt and without being burnt." The scholarly monarch Francis I of France chose as his emblem a salamander in flames with the motto: "I nourish and extinguish."

But the mythical lizard gained enduring magical significance in the Renaissance, when Paracelsus, the great Swiss magus, declared the salamander to be the Elemental of Fire. The doctrine of Paracelsus held that Elementals were primal beings inhabiting the classical four roots of matter: gnomes of Earth, sylphs of Air, and undines of Water. The salamander of Fire symbolically expressed a spark igniting action, purification, and transformation. Paracelsus equated the essence of fire with the power of imagination in the human spirit: "that explosive flare that lights up the inner spaces, revealing meaning."

No great leap of imagination is required to guess the origin of the fabulous salamander, given the zoological creature's actual habits. The tiny lizard likes to cozy up in a log with a nice damp hole. And if such a log turns up in a fireplace and the salamander is rudely awakened by flames, its movements are less frolic than frantic, a usually successful scramble for life. Young Cellini undoubtedly reported what he saw correctly and took a blow to remember the fiery little dragon surviving despite all odds. The memory served Cellini well, for he managed to keep a cool head in a hotbed of court intrigues, all the while producing beautiful art in his wild and wonderful career.

Selkies

BELOW the chilly waters of the Shetland and Orkney Islands lived the Selkies, strange seal people who inhabited a netherworld below the depths of the sea. They were fallen angels, the Scots believed, banished to the sea for their sins but allowed human form on dry land. They enjoyed donning sealskins from head to toe and swimming upward from one region of air to another, where they shed their soft fur and sometimes pleasantly encountered mortals.

The strange creatures were extraordinarily beautiful, as befits angels, and women became wildly enchanted by Selkie men at a glance. The amorous seal creatures enjoyed making love to human women and made expeditions to that purpose, but seldom stayed long. Male Selkies tended to seduce and abandon, even as some mortal counterparts. But Ursilla, a passionate island woman, kept one close for years. Discontented with her fisherman husband, she invoked a Selkie by sitting on a rock at high tide and dropping seven tears into the sea. A lover duly arrived and returned often enough to father numerous offspring, all of whom had webbed hands and feet.

Selkie women had a different story. They loved dancing as much as their cousins the mermaids loved singing, shedding their sealskins and cavorting nude on beaches. The divinely graceful dancer with pearly skin, legs flashing and golden hair flying, was a riveting sight for mortal man, set immediately aflame with desire. The island men had learned that if they stole the sealskin and hid it, the beauty became a reluctant captive — but would nonetheless serve as a fond but somewhat sad wife and mother. She would roam the beaches at high tide during the Full Moon, all dance vanished from her limbs, nostalgic for her undersea realm and Selkie husband. She never stopped searching for the sealskin, and if she found the hidden fur she would slip it on and streak downward to reunite with her first love, her true love. And that is probably as things should be.

Mermaids and Selkies have a great mutual tenderness nurtured through an ancient myth: A young fisherman had stunned and skinned a Selkie, throwing her body into the water and pretending to the other fishermen that he had found a dead seal. But the Selkie was still alive, although gravely injured, and regained consciousness in the sea. Cold and pitiful, she found her way into an underwater cave inhabited by a mermaid. Touched by the plight of the Selkie, the mermaid swam upward to try regaining the Selkie's sealskin. In the boat where the sealskin lay she permitted herself to be caught in the net, to the stupefaction of the crew. Remorseful at his destruction of the seal the young fisherman tried to free the mermaid, but the others were determined to take the rarity ashore and sell this most valuable of finny creatures.

The poor mermaid, still tangled in the lines, was laid on the sealskin and the boat sped toward shore. But mermaids cannot long endure the upper air, and her life was ebbing. She knew that Selkie men would exact revenge by sending a gale and sinking the ship. The mermaid's last wish was that the skin would sink with her body down to the cave. That is how it happened. The Selkie, grieving for her brave friend, slipped on her sealskin, revived shortly and dove down, down to her natural element.

Since that time Selkies have been loving toward mermaids, and will risk their lives to provide them protection.

How do we know this? Perhaps a mermaid sang the tale to a mortal who passed it down.

Unicorns

OF ALL the creatures in the Zoo of the Fabulous, the unicorn is perhaps the most beautiful. It is a horse slightly larger than the real thing, perfectly formed on its slim legs, eyes blue as sapphires, from its forehead arising a long horn with a red tip like a little flame. The unicorn ambles its way through the forest, a flash of gleaming white amid the greenery.

But such glamour is a modern concept. In its mythological onset the unicorn is an outlandish creature as described by the Roman naturalist Pliny. He assures us that it is "similar in the rest of its body to a horse, with the head of a deer, the feet of an elephant, the tail of a boar." It is a "very ferocious beast," he says, and cannot be taken alive. Perhaps that explained to the populace why unicorns found no place in the Coliseum among the thousands of lions, panthers and rhinos slaughtered in lethal entertainments. The Chinese also recognized the unicorn as an odd assembly of body parts, calling it "the four-not-like" — the body of a horse but not like a horse, the feet of an antelope but not like an antelope, the head of a deer but not like a deer, the tail of a boar but not like a boar.

Hunters considered unicorns prize game, but were sorely puzzled about how to overcome such fierce creatures. They believed that the horn functioned like a small sword, movable at the animal's will, and only a fine fencer could survive the bizarre duel. Others maintained that the sword had magical strength, and that the pursued unicorn could throw itself over a cliff, land on its horn, and canter away unscathed. During the Middle Ages, the myth spins off in another fanciful direction. The unicorn was a great lover of purity, it was believed, and powerfully attracted to virginal innocence. Hunters began taking to the field with maidens, who would sit in conspicuous sites. When the unicorn spied the girl, it would approach with all reverence, lay its head gently on her lap and fall asleep. The treacherous maiden would then signal hunters, who would seize the beast. Artists loved the visual appeal of the story, and the unicorn hunt turns up in widespread medieval works from Europe, the Islamic world and China.

Throughout the ages and shifting stories people believed that the horn had magical properties. Dipping a horn into water purified the drink. Stomach trouble and epilepsy vanished at a swig of unicorn-horn elixir. Medieval kings and popes owned unicorn horns and used them as amulets to detect poisons in their food. As late as the 16th century the horns were used as very expensive antidotes.

By about that time belief in the unicorn dwindles and disappears, although in 1673 a Dr. Olfert Dapper reports spotting one in the Maine woods. And a unicorn turns up in the Lewis Carroll children's classic. At their encounter Alice says, "Do you know, I always thought unicorns were fabulous monsters. I never saw one alive before!"

"Well, now that we have seen each other," said the Unicorn, "if you'll believe in me, I'll believe in you. Is that a bargain?"

"Yes, if you like," said Alice. And that seems fair enough.

In the beginning of all things, wisdom and knowledge were with the animals; for Tirawa, the One Above, did not speak directly to man. He sent certain animals to tell man that he showed himself through the beasts, and that from them, and from the stars and the sun and the moon, man should learn. Tirawa spoke to man through his works.

— CHIEF LETAKOTS-LESA